MW01610267

Amazing Ideas To Crochet Hats

Simple and Beautiful Pattern To Try

Copyright © 2022

All rights reserved.

DEDICATION

Contents

Texture Hat

Supplies

Yarn: Red Heart Super Saver Ombre, 100 % Acrylic, (10 oz / 283 g; 482 yds/ 440 m), [4] Medium Weight Yarn, Color: True Blue (Yarn Care: Machine Wash and Dry)

Hook: 5.5 mm (I) Clover Amour

Scissors, Yarn Needle, Stitch Marker (optional)

Difficulty Level

Easy (although a dedicated beginner should be able to master this one too!)

Finished Size

See sizes in the pattern instructions below.

Gauge

approximately 13 post stitches worked in pattern stitch in 4 inches

approximately 12 rounds worked in pattern stitch in 4 inches

You can substitute any yarn and hook for this stitch pattern – just remember when you substitute if your gauge is different, the finished size of your project will also be different.

Abbreviations

US Terminology used

BPdc – back post double crochet

ch – chain

dc – double crochet

FPdc – front post double crochet

MR – magic ring

R – row

rem – remaining

rep – repeat

sc – single crochet

sk – skip

st/sts – stitch/stitches

* – Repeat the instructions between the asterisks the number of times indicated. This repeat will contain of multiple instructions.

() – Repeat the instructions between the parentheses the number of times indicated.

[] – at the end of the row – the total number of stitches

Notes

This project is worked in rounds.

do not count the sl st as a stitch

do not count the ch 3 at the beginning of a round as a stitch

do not count the ch 2 at the beginning of a round as a stitch

the first st of each round is worked in the same st as you sl st to join

length of hat is to the base of the earlobe; instructions have been included for mid-ear length as well.

This stitch pattern is not super stretchy, so for the smaller sizes I have allowed 1 inch negative ease (I normally allow 2 inches for stretchier hat designs). I wanted to make sure the hats were easy to put on for little ones and for soft spots on babies heads. I am not sure this would be a good hat for preemies; therefore, I have not included the preemie size in this pattern. I am concerned the added texture might actually be uncomfortable for their softer skin and level of skull development.

Pattern Instructions

Newborn

Finished hat size: 13" circumference, 5" height. To fit 14" head size.

R1: MR: ch 3, 12 dc, sl st to the top of first dc to join. [12]

R2: Ch 3, 2 dc in each st around; sl st to the first dc to join. [24]

R3: Ch 3,*2 dc in the next st, 1 dc in the next st**. Rep from * to ** 12 times. Sl st to the first dc to join. [36]

R4: Ch 3,*2 dc in the next st, 1 dc in each of the next 2 sts**. Rep from * to ** 8 times. 1 dc in each rem st around. Sl st to the first dc to join. [44]

R5: Ch 2, *1 FPdc in each of the next 2 sts, 1 BPdc in each of the next 2 sts**. Rep from * to ** around. Sl st to the first dc to join. [44]

R6: Ch 2, *1 BPdc in each of the next 2 sts, 1 FPdc in each of the next 2 sts**. Rep from * to ** around. Sl st to the first dc to join. [44]

R7-15: Rep R5 and R6

R16: 1 sc in each st around. [44 sc]

R17: 1 sc in BL of each st around. Finish off with an invisible join and weave in ends. [44 sc]

If you would prefer the hat to reach mid ear, stop your repeats after Round 13 and then continue to R16 and R17 to complete the hat.

0-3 months

Finished hat size: 15" circumference, 6" height. To fit 16" head size.

R1: MR: ch 3, 12 dc, sl st to the top of first dc to join. [12]

R2: Ch 3, 2 dc in each st around; sl st to the first dc to join. [24]

R3: Ch 3,*2 dc in the next st, 1 dc in the next st**. Rep from * to ** 12 times. Sl st to the first dc to join. [36]

R4: Ch 3,*2 dc in the next st, 1 dc in each of the next 2 sts**. Rep from * to ** 12 times. Sl st to the first dc to join. [48]

R5: Ch 2, *1 FPdc in each of the next 2 sts, 1 BPdc in each of the next 2 sts**. Rep from * to ** around. Sl st to the first dc to join. [48]

R6: Ch 2, *1 BPdc in each of the next 2 sts, 1 FPdc in each of the next 2 sts**. Rep from * to ** around. Sl st to the first dc to join. [48]

R7-18: Rep R5 and R6

R19: 1 sc in each st around. [52 sc]

R20: 1 sc in BL of each st around. Finish off with an invisible join and weave in ends. [52 sc]

If you would prefer the hat to reach mid ear, stop your repeats after Round 16 and then continue to R19 and R20 to complete the hat.

3 mos – 6 months

Finished hat size: 16" circumference, 6.25" height. To fit 17" head size.

R1: MR: ch 3, 12 dc, sl st to the top of first dc to join. [12]

R2: Ch 3, 2 dc in each st around; sl st to the first dc to join. [24]

R3: Ch 3,*2 dc in the next st, 1 dc in the next st**. Rep from * to ** 12 times. Sl st to the first dc to join. [36]

R4: Ch 3,*2 dc in the next st, 1 dc in each of the next 2 sts**. Rep from * to ** 12 times. Sl st to the first dc to join. [48]

R5: Ch 3, *2 dc in the next st, 1 dc in each of the next 3 sts**. Rep from * to ** 4 times. 1 dc in each rem st around. Sl st to the first dc to join. [52]

R6: Ch 2, *1 FPdc in each of the next 2 sts, 1 BPdc in each of the next 2 sts**. Rep from * to ** around. Sl st to the first dc to join. [52]

R7: Ch 2, *1 BPdc in each of the next 2 sts, 1 FPdc in each of the next 2 sts**. Rep from * to ** around. Sl st to the first dc to join. [52]

R8-19: Rep R6 and R7

R20: 1 sc in each st around. [52 sc]

R21: 1 sc in BL of each st around. Finish off with an invisible join and weave in ends. [52 sc]

If you would prefer the hat to reach mid ear, stop your repeats after Round 15 and then continue to R20 and R21 to complete the hat.

6 mos – 12 months

Finished hat size: 17" circumference, 6.75" height. To fit 18" head size.

R1: MR: ch 3, 12 dc, sl st to the top of first dc to join. [12]

R2: Ch 3, 2 dc in each st around; sl st to the first dc to join. [24]

R3: Ch 3,*2 dc in the next st, 1 dc in the next st**. Rep from * to ** 12 times. Sl st to the first dc to join. [36]

R4: Ch 3,*2 dc in the next st, 1 dc in each of the next 2 sts**. Rep from * to ** 12 times. Sl st to the first dc to join. [48]

R5: Ch 3, *2 dc in the next st, 1 dc in each of the next 3 sts**. Rep from * to ** 8 times. 1 dc in each rem st around. Sl st to the first dc to join. [56]

R6: Ch 2, *1 FPdc in each of the next 2 sts, 1 BPdc in each of the next 2 sts**. Rep from * to ** around. Sl st to the first dc to join. [56]

R7: Ch 2, *1 BPdc in each of the next 2 sts, 1 FPdc in each of the next 2 sts**. Rep from * to ** around. Sl st to the first dc to join. [56]

R8-21: Rep R6 and R7

R21: 1 sc in each st around. [56 sc]

R22: 1 sc in BL of each st around. Finish off with an invisible join and weave in ends. [56 sc]

If you would prefer the hat to reach mid ear, stop your repeats after Round 16 and then continue to R21 and R22 to complete the hat.

12 mos – 24 months

Finished hat size: 18" circumference, 7" height. To fit 19" head size.

R1: MR: ch 3, 12 dc, sl st to the top of first dc to join. [12]

R2: Ch 3, 2 dc in each st around; sl st to the first dc to join. [24]

R3: Ch 3,*2 dc in the next st, 1 dc in the next st**. Rep from * to ** 12 times. Sl st to the first dc to join. [36]

R4: Ch 3,*2 dc in the next st, 1 dc in each of the next 2 sts**. Rep from * to ** 12 times. Sl st to the first dc to join. [48]

R5: Ch 3, *2 dc in the next st, 1 dc in each of the next 3 sts**. Rep from * to ** 12 times. Sl st to the first dc to join. [60]

R6: Ch 2, *1 FPdc in each of the next 2 sts, 1 BPdc in each of the next 2 sts**. Rep from * to ** around. Sl st to the first dc to join. [60]

R7: Ch 2, *1 BPdc in each of the next 2 sts, 1 FPdc in each of the next 2 sts**. Rep from * to ** around. Sl st to the first dc to join. [60]

R8-20: Rep R6 and R7

R21: 1 sc in each st around. [60 sc]

R22: 1 sc in BL of each st around. Finish off with an invisible join and weave in ends. [60 sc]

If you would prefer the hat to reach mid ear, stop your repeats after Round 17 and then continue to R21 and R22 to complete the hat.

Toddler (3-5 years)

Finished hat size: 19" circumference, 7.5 " height. To fit 20" head size.

R1: MR: ch 3, 12 dc, sl st to the top of first dc to join. [12]

R2: Ch 3, 2 dc in each st around; sl st to the first dc to join. [24]

R3: Ch 3,*2 dc in the next st, 1 dc in the next st**. Rep from * to ** 12 times. Sl st to the first dc to join. [36]

R4: Ch 3,*2 dc in the next st, 1 dc in each of the next 2 sts**. Rep from * to ** 12 times. Sl st to the first dc to join. [48]

R5: Ch 3, *2 dc in the next st, 1 dc in each of the next 3 sts**. Rep from * to ** 12 times. Sl st to the first dc to join. [60]

R6: Ch 3, *2 dc in the next st, 1 dc in each of the next 4 sts**. Rep from * to ** 4 times. 1 dc in each rem st around. Sl st to the first dc to join. [64]

R7: Ch 2, *1 FPdc in each of the next 2 sts, 1 BPdc in each of the next 2 sts**. Rep from * to ** around. Sl st to the first dc to join. [64]

R8: Ch 2, *1 BPdc in each of the next 2 sts, 1 FPdc in each of the next 2 sts**. Rep from * to ** around. Sl st to the first dc to join. [64]

R9-21: Rep R7 and R8

R22: 1 sc in each st around. [64 sc]

R23: 1 sc in BL of each st around. Finish off with an invisible join and weave in ends. [64 sc]

If you would prefer the hat to reach mid ear, stop your repeats after Round 20 and then continue to R22 and R23 to complete the hat.

Child (7-10 years)

Finished hat size: 20" circumference, 8 " height. To fit 21" head size.

R1: MR: ch 3, 12 dc, sl st to the top of first dc to join. [12]

R2: Ch 3, 2 dc in each st around; sl st to the first dc to join. [24]

R3: Ch 3,*2 dc in the next st, 1 dc in the next st**. Rep from * to ** 12 times. Sl st to the first dc to join. [36]

R4: Ch 3,*2 dc in the next st, 1 dc in each of the next 2 sts**. Rep from * to ** 12 times. Sl st to the first dc to join. [48]

R5: Ch 3, *2 dc in the next st, 1 dc in each of the next 3 sts**. Rep from * to ** 12 times. Sl st to the first dc to join. [60]

R6: Ch 3, *2 dc in the next st, 1 dc in each of the next 4 sts**. Rep from * to ** 8 times. 1 dc in each rem st around. Sl st to the first dc to join. [68]

R7: Ch 2, *1 FPdc in each of the next 2 sts, 1 BPdc in each of the next 2 sts**. Rep from * to ** around. Sl st to the first dc to join. [68]

R8: Ch 2, *1 BPdc in each of the next 2 sts, 1 FPdc in each of the next 2 sts**. Rep from * to ** around. Sl st to the first dc to join. [68]

R9-22: Rep R7 and R8

R23: 1 sc in each st around. [68 sc]

R24: 1 sc in BL of each st around. Finish off with an invisible join and weave in ends. [68 sc]

If you would prefer the hat to reach mid ear, stop your repeats after Round 20 and then continue to R23 and R24 to complete the hat.

Small Adult (Teen)

Finished hat size: 20" circumference, 8.25 " height. To fit 22" head size.

R1: MR: ch 3, 12 dc, sl st to the top of first dc to join. [12]

R2: Ch 3, 2 dc in each st around; sl st to the first dc to join. [24]

R3: Ch 3,*2 dc in the next st, 1 dc in the next st**. Rep from * to ** 12 times. Sl st to the first dc to join. [36]

R4: Ch 3,*2 dc in the next st, 1 dc in each of the next 2 sts**. Rep from * to ** 12 times. Sl st to the first dc to join. [48]

R5: Ch 3, *2 dc in the next st, 1 dc in each of the next 3 sts**. Rep from * to ** 12 times. Sl st to the first dc to join. [60]

R6: Ch 3, *2 dc in the next st, 1 dc in each of the next 4 sts**. Rep from * to ** 8 times. 1 dc in each rem st around. Sl st to the first dc to join. [68]

R7: Ch 2, *1 FPdc in each of the next 2 sts, 1 BPdc in each of the next 2 sts**. Rep from * to ** around. Sl st to the first dc to join. [68]

R8: Ch 2, *1 BPdc in each of the next 2 sts, 1 FPdc in each of the next 2 sts**. Rep from * to ** around. Sl st to the first dc to join. [68]

R9-23: Rep R7 and R8

R24: 1 sc in each st around. [68 sc]

R25: 1 sc in BL of each st around. Finish off with an invisible join and weave in ends. [68 sc]

If you would prefer the hat to reach mid ear, stop your repeats after Round 21 and then continue to R24 and R25 to complete the hat.

Medium Adult (Woman)

Finished hat size: 21" circumference, 8.75 " height. To fit 23" head size.

R1: MR: ch 3, 12 dc, sl st to the top of first dc to join. [12]

R2: Ch 3, 2 dc in each st around; sl st to the first dc to join. [24]

R3: Ch 3,*2 dc in the next st, 1 dc in the next st**. Rep from * to **

12 times. Sl st to the first dc to join. [36]

R4: Ch 3,*2 dc in the next st, 1 dc in each of the next 2 sts**. Rep from * to ** 12 times. Sl st to the first dc to join. [48]

R5: Ch 3, *2 dc in the next st, 1 dc in each of the next 3 sts**. Rep from * to ** 12 times. Sl st to the first dc to join. [60]

R6: Ch 3, *2 dc in the next st, 1 dc in each of the next 4 sts**. Rep from * to ** 12 times. Sl st to the first dc to join. [72]

R7: Ch 2, *1 FPdc in each of the next 2 sts, 1 BPdc in each of the next 2 sts**. Rep from * to ** around. Sl st to the first dc to join. [72]

R8: Ch 2, *1 BPdc in each of the next 2 sts, 1 FPdc in each of the next 2 sts**. Rep from * to ** around. Sl st to the first dc to join. [72]

R9-24: Rep R7 and R8

R25: 1 sc in each st around. [72 sc]

R26: 1 sc in BL of each st around. Finish off with an invisible join and weave in ends. [72 sc]

If you would prefer the hat to reach mid ear, stop your repeats after Round 23 and then continue to R25 and R26 to complete the hat.

Large Adult (Men)

Finished hat size: 22" circumference, 9" height. To fit 24" head size.

R1: MR: ch 3, 12 dc, sl st to the top of first dc to join. [12]

R2: Ch 3, 2 dc in each st around; sl st to the first dc to join. [24]

R3: Ch 3,*2 dc in the next st, 1 dc in the next st**. Rep from * to ** 12 times. Sl st to the first dc to join. [36]

R4: Ch 3,*2 dc in the next st, 1 dc in each of the next 2 sts**. Rep from * to ** 12 times. Sl st to the first dc to join. [48]

R5: Ch 3, *2 dc in the next st, 1 dc in each of the next 3 sts**. Rep from * to ** 12 times. Sl st to the first dc to join. [60]

R6: Ch 3, *2 dc in the next st, 1 dc in each of the next 4 sts**. Rep from * to ** 12 times. Sl st to the first dc to join. [72]

R7: Ch 3, *2 dc in the next st, 1 dc in each of the next 5 sts**. Rep from * to ** 2 times. 1 dc in each rem st around. Sl st to the first dc to join. [74]

R8: Ch 2, *1 FPdc in each of the next 2 sts, 1 BPdc in each of the next 2 sts**. Rep from * to ** around. Sl st to the first dc to join. [74]

R9: Ch 2, *1 BPdc in each of the next 2 sts, 1 FPdc in each of the next 2 sts**. Rep from * to ** around. Sl st to the first dc to join. [74]

R10-25: Rep R8 and R9

R26: 1 sc in each st around. [74 sc]

R27: 1 sc in BL of each st around. Finish off with an invisible join and weave in ends. [74 sc]

If you would prefer the hat to reach mid ear, stop your repeats after Round 24 and then continue to R26 and R27 to complete the hat.

Crochet Owl Hat Pattern

Supplies:

• Vanna's Choice® Lion Brand medium worsted weight yarn (I use Barley and an accent color such as pink, green, purple, turquoise)

• Crochet hook size H-8 (5.0 mm)

• Tapestry needle for weaving in ends

• Two 3/4" black button for eyes

Abbreviations:

ch – chain

sl st- slip stitch

SC – Single Crochet

DC – Double Crochet

HDC – Half Double Crochet

HDC Decrease – Half Double Crochet Decrease

TC – Triple Crochet

Gauge:

4" across = 14 double crochet stitches

4" height = 8 rows of double crochets

Note: I have simplified this pattern since writing the newborn size so you may notice the larger sizes start differently and have a different stitch count but in the end they will look the same.

Size: 3-6 Months

Magic Ring, Chain 2, 9 DC in magic ring, join to first DC, ch 2

Round 2: 2 DC in each around, join to first DC, ch 2 (18 DC)

Round 3: 2 DC, DC in next, repeat around, join, ch 2 (27 DC)

Round 4: 2 DC, DC in next 2, repeat around, join, ch 2 (36 DC)

Round 5: 2 DC, DC in next 3, repeat around, join, ch 2 (45 DC)

Round 6: DC around (45 DC)

Change color, join and ch 2

Round 7-10: DC around (45 DC)

do not fasten off, begin on first earflap as written below for this size

Size: 6-12 Months:

Magic Ring, Chain 2, 9 DC in magic ring, join to first DC, ch 2

Round 2: 2 DC in each around, join to first DC, ch 2 (18 DC)

Round 3: 2 DC, DC in next, repeat around, join, ch 2 (27 DC)

Round 4: 2 DC, DC in next 2, repeat around, join, ch 2 (36 DC)

Round 5: 2 DC, DC in next 3, repeat around, join, ch 2 (45 DC)

Round 6: 2 DC, DC in next 8, repeat around, join, ch 2 (50 DC)

Round 7: DC around (50 DC)

Change Color, join and ch 2

Round 8-11: DC around (50 DC)

do not fasten off, begin on first earflap as written below for this size

Size: Toddler/Preschooler

Magic Ring, Chain 2, 9 DC in magic ring, join to first DC, ch 2

Round 2: 2 DC in each around, join to first DC, ch 2 (18 DC)

Round 3: 2 DC, DC in next, repeat around, join, ch 2 (27 DC)

Round 4: 2 DC, DC in next 2, repeat around, join, ch 2 (36 DC)

Round 5: 2 DC, DC in next 3, repeat around, join, ch 2 (45 DC)

Round 6: 2 DC, DC in next 4, repeat around, join, ch 2 (54 DC)

Round 7: DC around (54 DC)

Change color, join and ch 2

Round 8-12: DC around (54 DC) do not fasten off, begin on first earflap as written below for this size

Size: Child

Magic Ring, Chain 2, 9 DC in magic ring, join to first DC, ch 2

Round 2: 2 DC in each around, join to first DC, ch 2 (18 DC)

Round 3: 2 DC in first stitch, DC in next, repeat around, join, ch 2 (27 DC)

Round 4: 2 DC in first stitch, DC in next 2, repeat around, join, ch 2 (36 DC)

Round 5: 2 DC in first stitch, DC in next 3, repeat around, join, ch 2

(45 DC)

Round 6: 2 DC in first stitch, DC in next 4, repeat around, join, ch 2 (54 DC)

Round 7: DC around (54 DC)

Round 8: 2 DC in first stitch, DC in next 8, repeat around (60 DC)

Change color, join and ch 2

Round 9-13: DC around (60 DC)

do not fasten off, begin on first earflap as written below for this size

Size: Teen/Adult

Magic Ring, Chain 2, 9 DC in magic ring, join to first DC, ch 2

Round 2: 2 DC in each around, join to first DC, ch 2 (18 DC)

Round 3: 2 DC in first stitch, DC in next, repeat around, join, ch 2 (27 DC)

Round 4: 2 DC in first stitch, DC in next 2, repeat around, join, ch 2 (36 DC)

Round 5: 2 DC in first stitch, DC in next 3, repeat around, join, ch 2 (45 DC)

Round 6: 2 DC in first stitch, DC in next 4, repeat around, join, ch 2 (54 DC)

Round 7: DC around (54 DC)

Round 8: 2 Dc in first stitch, DC in next 8, repeat around, join, ch 2 (60 DC)

Round 9: 2 DC, DC in next 29, repeat around (62 DC)

Change color, join and ch 2

Round 10-14: DC around (62 DC)

do not fasten off, begin on first earflap

Size: Large Adult

Magic Ring, Chain 2, 9 DC in magic ring, join to first DC, ch 2

Round 2: 2 DC in each around, join to first DC, ch 2 (18 DC)

Round 3: 2 DC in first stitch, DC in next, repeat around, join, ch 2 (27 DC)

Round 4: 2 DC in first stitch, DC in next 2, repeat around, join, ch 2

(36 DC)

Round 5: 2 DC in first stitch, DC in next 3, repeat around, join, ch 2 (45 DC)

Round 6: 2 DC in first stitch, DC in next 4, repeat around, join, ch 2 (54 DC)

Round 7: DC around (54 DC)

Round 8: 2 Dc in first stitch, DC in next 8, repeat around, join, ch 2 (60 DC)

Round 9: 2 DC, DC in next 9, repeat around (66 DC)

Change color, join and ch 2

Round 10-15: DC around (66 DC)

do not fasten off, begin on first earflap

****

Earflaps for 3-6 month, 6-12 month, Toddler/Preschooler:

Earflap 1:

Row 1: Chain 2, HDC 10, chain 2, turn

Row 2: HDC decrease, HDC in next 6, HDC decrease chain 2, turn

Row 3: HDC across, chain 2, turn (8 HDC)

Row 4: HDC decrease, HDC in next 4, HDC decrease, chain 2, turn

Row 5: HDC across, chain 2, turn (6 HDC)

Row 6: HDC decrease, HDC in next 2, HDC decrease, chain 2, turn

Row 7: 2 HDC decreases, chain 2, turn

Row 8: HDC decrease, fasten off leaving long tail.

Earflap 2:

Leaving 15 stitches along the front for 3-6 month, 18 stitches along the front for 6-12 month, and 20 stitches along the front for Toddler/Preschooler …

Row 1: Chain 2, HDC 10, chain 2, turn

Row 2: HDC decrease, HDC in next 6, HDC decrease, chain 2, turn

Row 3: HDC across, chain 2, turn (8 HDC)

Row 4: HDC decrease, HDC in next 4, HDC decrease, chain 2, turn

Row 5: HDC across, chain 2, turn (6 HDC)

Row 6: HDC decrease, HDC in next 2, HDC decrease, chain 2, turn

Row 7: 2 HDC decreases, chain 2, turn

Row 8: HDC decrease, chain 1, turn

Continue to SC around the entire hat. Join to first SC and fasten off, leaving long tail.

****

Earflaps for Child and Teen/Adult:

Earflap 1:

Row 1: Chain 2, HDC 12, chain 2, turn

Row 2: HDC decrease, HDC in next 8, HDC decrease, chain 2, turn

Row 3: HDC across, chain 2, turn (10 HDC)

Row 4: HDC decrease, HDC in next 6, HDC decrease, chain 2, turn

Row 5: HDC across, chain 2, turn (8 HDC)

Row 6: HDC decrease, HDC in next 4, HDC decrease, chain 2, turn

Row 7: HDC across, chain 2, turn (6 HDC)

Row 8: HDC decrease, HDC in next 2, HDC decrease, chain 2, turn

Row 9: 2 HDC decreases, chain 2, turn

Row 10: HDC decrease, fasten off leaving long tail.

Earflap 2:

Leaving 23 stitches along the front for child size hat, 25 stitches along the front for adult size hat...

Row 1: Chain 2, HDC 12, chain 2, turn

Row 2: HDC decrease, HDC in next 8, HDC decrease, chain 2, turn

Row 3: HDC across, chain 2, turn (10 HDC)

Row 4: HDC decrease, HDC in next 6, HDC decrease, chain 2, turn

Row 5: HDC across, chain 2, turn (8 HDC)

Row 6: HDC decrease, HDC in next 4, HDC decrease, chain 2, turn

Row 7: HDC across, chain 2, turn (6 HDC)

Row 8: HDC decrease, HDC in next 2, HDC decrease, chain 2, turn

Row 9: 2 HDC decreases, chain 2, turn

Row 10: HDC decrease, chain 1, turn

Continue to SC around the entire hat. Join to first SC and fasten off, leaving long tail.

****

Eyes (Make 2):

In first color (this is your accent color):

Magic Ring, Chain 2

Round 1: 10 DC in magic ring, Change color to white before joining to first DC, chain 2 (10)

Round 2: 2 DC in same stitch and in each stitch around, join, chain 1 (20)

Round 3: SC in same stitch, 2 SC in next, *SC, 2 SC in next, repeat from * around, join to first sc, fasten off leaving long tail to sew on (30) After sewing crocheted eyes on, sew 3/4" black button in the center for the eyeballs

****

Nose:

Small nose:

Chain 5

Slip stitch in 2nd chain from hook, SC, HDC, DC, fasten off leaving long tail to sew on

Medium nose:

Chain 6

Slip stitch in 2nd chain from hook, SC, HDC, DC, DC, fasten off leaving long tail to sew on

Large nose:

Chain 7

Slip stitch in 2nd chain from hook, SC, HDC, DC, DC, TC fasten off leaving long tail to sew on

****

Ears:

Cut two strands of 12 inch long pieces of yarn in each color (6 strands total).

Loop through 2 DC's in the crease of the 3rd round.

Knot and trim to approx 1"

****

Braided Tails:

Cut three 1 yard strands of each color (9 strands total).

Pass through last space in earflap. You should now have 18 strands to braid with.

Make knot and braid approx 5.5 inches long, knot, trim ends.

Unforgettable Hat

This hat took less than one skein. You can easily make it more slouchy by adding rounds. It actually ended up a little too slouchy for my taste, but it's okay. If you want it more fitted just crochet about 14 rounds instead of 16...or however many you need. It's easy to adjust.

Materials

Worsted Weight Yarn (I used Red Heart Boutique Unforgettable in Parrot)

I love Lion Brand Amazing as well (especially Mauna Loa colorway)

Size H (5mm) crochet hook

Yarn Needle

Gauge

15sts or 8 rows = 4 inches (10cm)

Pattern

Note: Join each round. Begin each round with ch 3 which will count as a dc.

Ch 4

Round 1: 11 dc in first chain made which will be the 4th ch from hook. The skipped three chains will count as the first dc. Join with sl st in top of first st of rnd. (12 dc)

Rnd 2: 2 dc in each st. Join (24 dc)

Rnd 3: 2 dc in first st, dc in next st. (2 dc in next st, dc in next st) around. Join (36 dc).

Rnd 4: 2 dc in first st, dc in next 2 sts. (2 dc in next st, dc in next 2 sts) around. Join (48 dc).

Rnd 5: 2 dc in first st, dc in next 3 sts. (2 dc in next st, dc in next 3 sts) around. Join (60 dc).

Rnd 6: 2 dc in first st, dc in next 4 sts. (2 dc in next st, dc in next 4 sts) around. Join (72 dc).

Rnds 7-16: Dc in each st around. Join. Do not finish off.

Work ribbing in rows. If you crochet loosely, go down a hook size to G. I crocheted the ribbing rather tightly, so the H hook worked fine for me.

Ch 12

Row 1: sc into one loop of each chain. You will be working back toward the body of the hat. (11 sc). Attach to hat with sl st into the next st on the hat. Sl st into the next st. Ch 1. Turn

Row 2: Skip over the ch and those slip stitches. Sc in the back loop only in each st across. Ch 1, turn. (11 sc) In the photo below, you can see where I skipped those sl sts and put the first sc in the back loop of the stitch that I'm holding.

Row 3: Sc in back loop only in each st across. Sl st into next 2 sts in the last rnd of the hat. Ch 1, turn.

In this photo you can see that I am attaching to the last round of the hat. Make sure you do not work into the same stitch that you already have a sl st in.

Rows 4- 71:   Repeat rows 2 and 3. It can be a little tricky at first to skip over those sl st made. Just count your stitches and make sure you only have 11 sc in each row. Remember those slip stitches are only to attach to the hat and not to work in to.

Keep going until you get all the way around.

Sl st into the last st on the hat and into the join. Now turn and sl st the seam together. I turned the hat inside out and slip stitched into the back loops of each of the joining rows.

Weave ends. All done!

Chunky Crochet Hat

If you want to make one for yourself or someone on your gift list, I will show you how!

CHUNKY CROCHET HAT SUPPLIES:

Size 5 Bulky Weight Yarn (I used one skein of Darice Folklore, you can also try Wool Ease Chunky, Paton's Classic Wool, Knit Picks Brava Bulky, or Lion Brand JiffyBulky.)

Size N (10.00 mm) Crochet Hook

Scissors

Yarn Needle

Pom Pom Maker (optional – you can also make pom poms just using your fingers OR try a faux fur pom pom)

CHUNKY CROCHET HAT PATTERN

Please note: This pattern is free for personal use. You may sell items you make using my patterns, but please use a link when possible. Pageviews help to support this blog and allow me to provide free patterns like this one. Thank you! ☺

This pattern uses American crochet terms.

First, you crochet a rectangle, sew it into a tube, and then close up the top; however, this had is topped off with a fluffy pom pom instead of the cute cat ears from last week's pattern. ☺

The hat's ribbed look is created by working half double crochet stitches into the back loops only. This means that rather than working the stitches under both strands of yarn at the top of the stitch, you will work the stitch only through the back strand as shown in the image below.

Row 1: Begin by chaining 23 and then working a half double crochet (hdc) stitch in the third chain from your hook and each remaining chain down the line. (The length of this first row is about an inch shorter than the finished hat will be brim to crown, so if you want your hat to be longer or shorter, you can adjust the crochet hat pattern

length by beginning again with more or fewer chains.) Chain 2, Turn.

Row 2: Working in the back loops only, work 1 hdc in each stitch across, Ch 2, turn.

Repeat Row 2 until your rectangle is long enough to wrap around your head. It took me 23 rows. You don't need to finish off the yarn yet.

Fold the rectangle in half so the two short ends of the rectangle line up. Work a slip stitch through each stitch of both sides to crochet the rectangle together into a tube.

When you have your tube, finish off the yarn and weave in the ends.

With the tube wrong side out (with the seam on the outside), thread a long piece of yarn onto your yarn needle and pull the needle through each row all around one end of the tube. Grab both ends of the yarn and pull tight to gather the top of the hat. Tie the ends together with a double knot and weave in the ends.

Finally, just flip the hat right side out, and – ta-da! – it's a hat! Well, kind of. It just needs a bit of finishing and then it will be awesome.

Adding a brim takes it to the next level. A few rounds of single crochet will do just fine.

Rnd 1: Join the yarn to the brim edge of the hat. Work single crochet stitches evenly around the edge. It took me 38 stitches to go all the way around. Slip stitch to the first single crochet to join. Chain 1.

Rnd 2: Working in back loops only (see image below), single crochet in each stitch around. Slip stitch to join. Chain 1.

Rnd 3: Repeat Round 2 leaving off the last chain 1. Finish off, weave in ends.

Last but not least, you can top the hat with a pom pom. I used the largest pom pom loom to make my fluffy pom pom, and then tied it onto the crown of the hat.

Fingers are great pom pom making tools too, OR a faux fur pom pom would also look pretty amazing. Right?

And that's it. Your new cozy hat is all ready to enjoy or gift. The ribbed stitch makes it nice and stretchy. It's long enough to leave it pushed back and slouchy or you can pull it down and fold up the brim.

55

Free Men's Crochet Hat Pattern

If you want to crochet a cold-weather hat for a special guy, this men's winter hat pattern is a great pattern for any crocheter. The hat is a classic style with a stitch that resembles a rib knit. But instead of knitting, this hat uses crochet. This hat is part of a coordinating set which also includes a winter scarf.

Crochet Skill Level

This crochet pattern is very easy. It's a great project for beginner crocheters who know the following basic stitches:

ch = chain

sc = single crochet

sl st = slip stitch

If you've ever done any simple hand sewing or embroidery, you'll have no problem with the finishing required for this project. And if those are new to you, you can still figure this out with ease.

Project Notes

The body of the hat starts with a rectangle, which you will use to create a tube shape. Then you gather the top of the tube with running stitch to close off the top of the hat.

Materials

Yarn: About 4 oz. of DK / light worsted weight wool yarn. The sample uses Knit Picks Swish DK in Lost Lake Heather

Crochet Hooks: Size K / 6.5 mm hook. Adjust the size if necessary to achieve the correct gauge.

Tapestry needle for weaving in ends.

Gauge

4 sts = 1 inch; row gauge is not important.

Be sure to make a gauge swatch before crocheting this hat.

Finished Size

This pattern fits an adult male. It measures approximately 11" long and 22" in circumference around the lower edge; it measures 11" across when laid flat.

If you'd like to make your hat longer than the sample, increase the number of chain stitches in your starting chain.

To make your hat shorter, decrease the number of chains in your starting chain.

If you'd like the hat to fit looser, crochet more rows.

To make it fit tighter, crochet fewer rows.

Men's Winter Crochet Hat Pattern

Ch 45.

Row 1: Sl st in 2nd ch from hook and in each ch st across the row. (44 sl sts.)

Row 2: Ch 1, turn. Work entire row in sl st. (44 sl sts.)

Row 3: Ch 1, turn. Work entire row in sl st. (44 sl sts.)

Row 4: Ch 1, turn. Work entire row in sc. (44 sc sts.)

Rows 5 and Up: Repeat rows 1–4 with the following minor change: on the first row of slip stitch after a row of single crochet, work the sl sts into the front loops of the sc sts in the previous row. Continue working in pattern repeat until your hat is the desired size.

A good gauge is to crochet 100 rows total, but you should crochet as many rows as necessary to achieve a comfortable fit for the intended wearer. You can do a quick fitting by using safety pins to pin up the sides of the hat and try it on.

Hold the active loop in place with a stitch marker and leave the yarn attached to the skein. Weave in the remaining ends. Block and let dry.

Finishing

With the right sides together, hold or pin the first and last row together to form a tube. Using the yarn still attached to the skein, work one slip stitch through both loops of both the stitches in the first row and last row.

Keep the hat turned wrong side out. Thread the yarn needle and hand stitch a loose running stitch all the way around the upper perimeter of the hat. Make the stitches as even as possible and near the edge. If the stitches are about 1" long, it makes it easier to close up the top of the hat.

Pull the running stitch to gather the top of the hat.

After pulling the gathers tight, make a few extra stitches to secure the gathers. Tie off the yarn.

If you aren't able to get the gathers pulled tight enough, you can also crochet a small circle and stitch it in place to close it off. However, before you do that, try restitching the top with larger stitches to get a tighter gather.

Turn the hat right side out and fold up the bottom brim.

Amazing Ideas To Crochet Hats

Made in the USA
Monee, IL
02 April 2023

31117845R10039